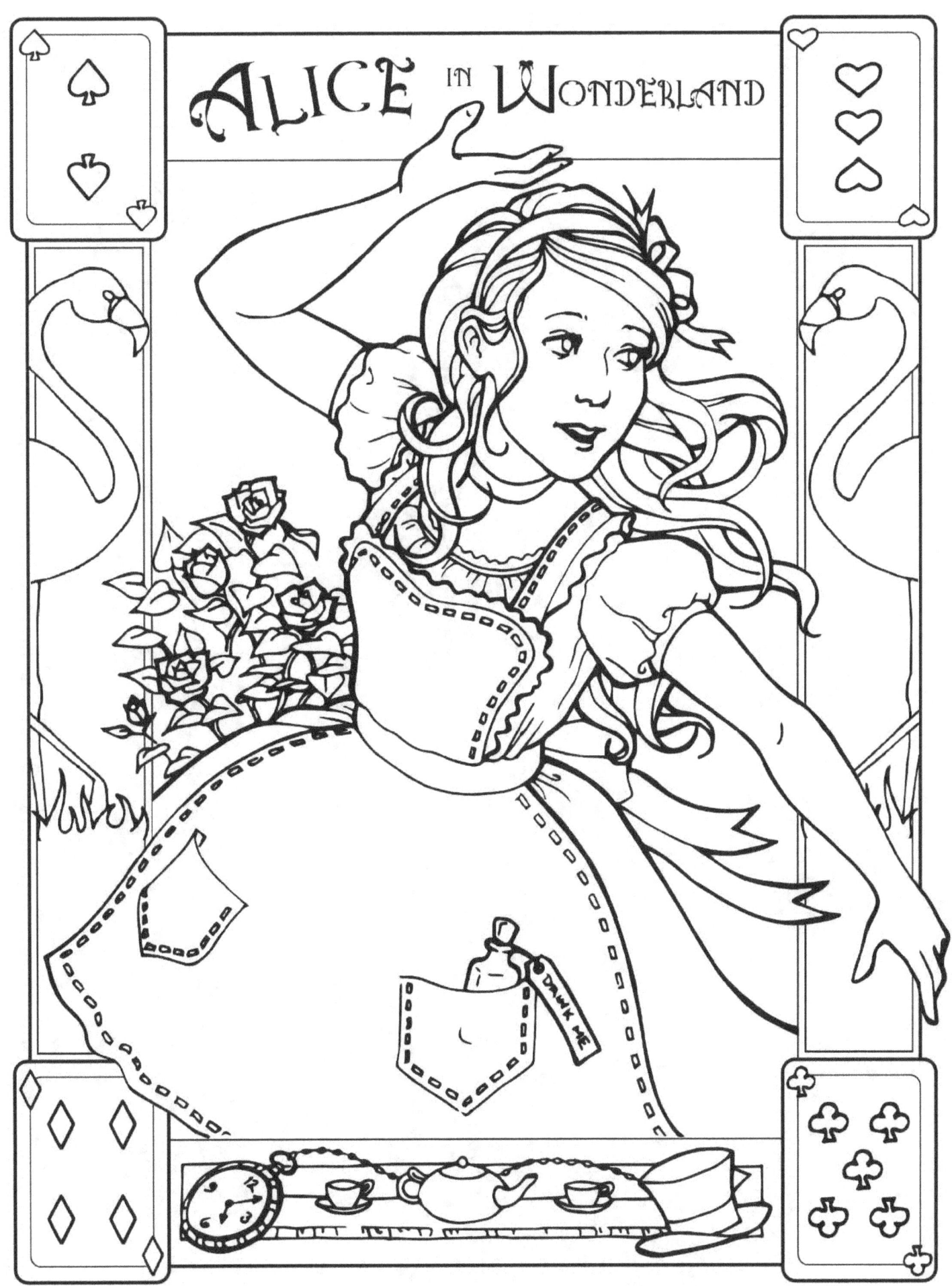

La Belle

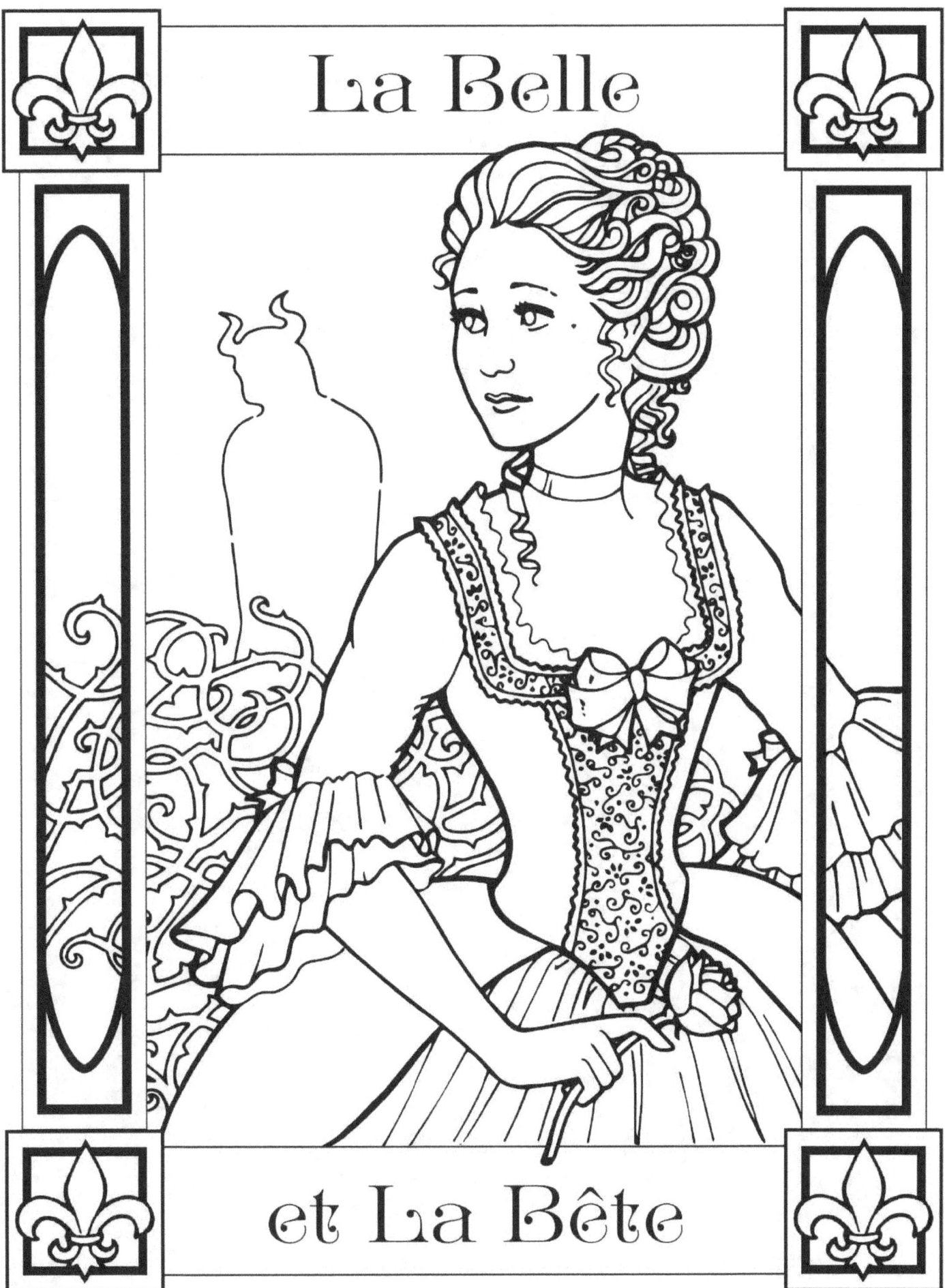

et La Bête

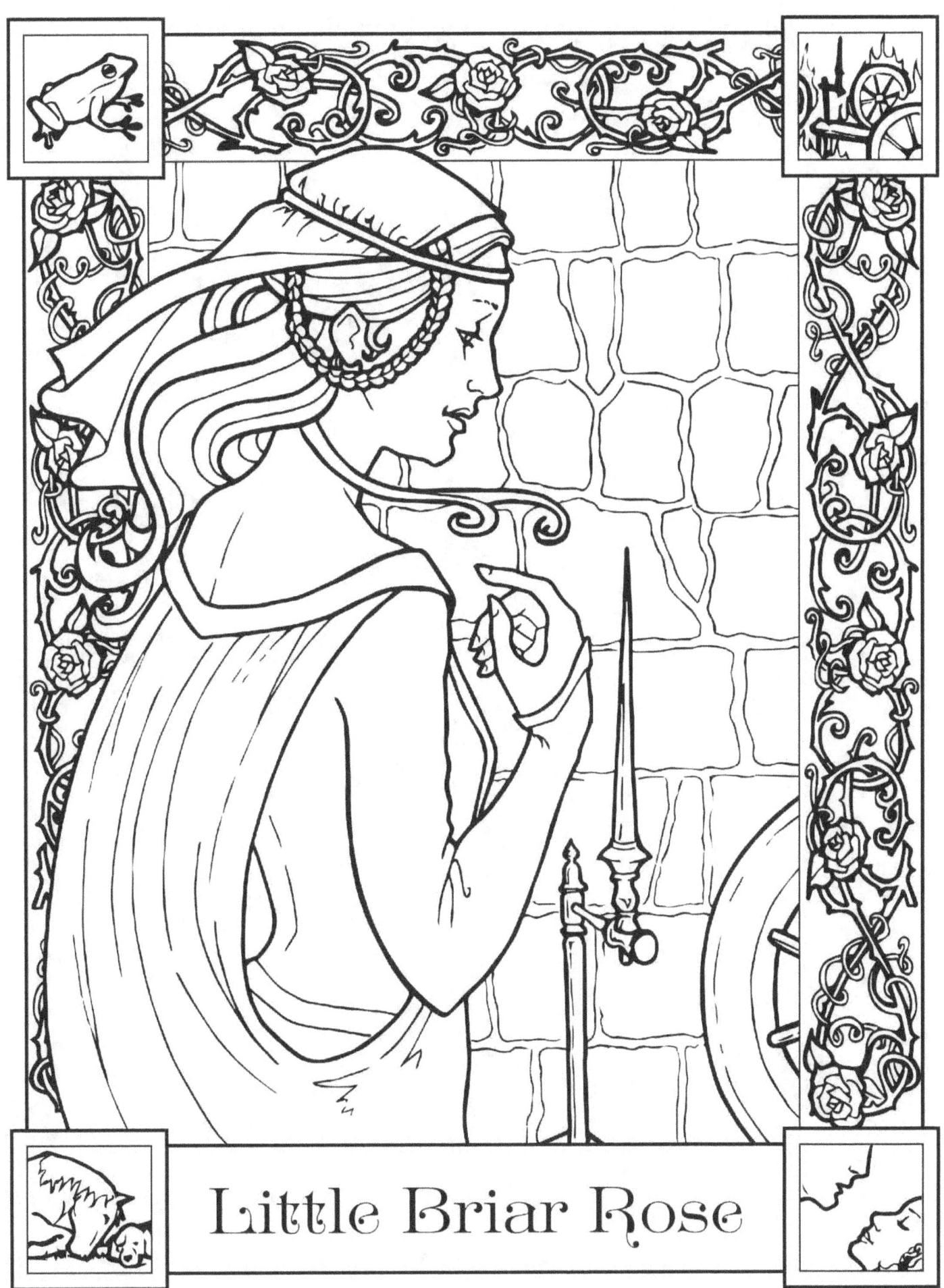

Little Briar Rose

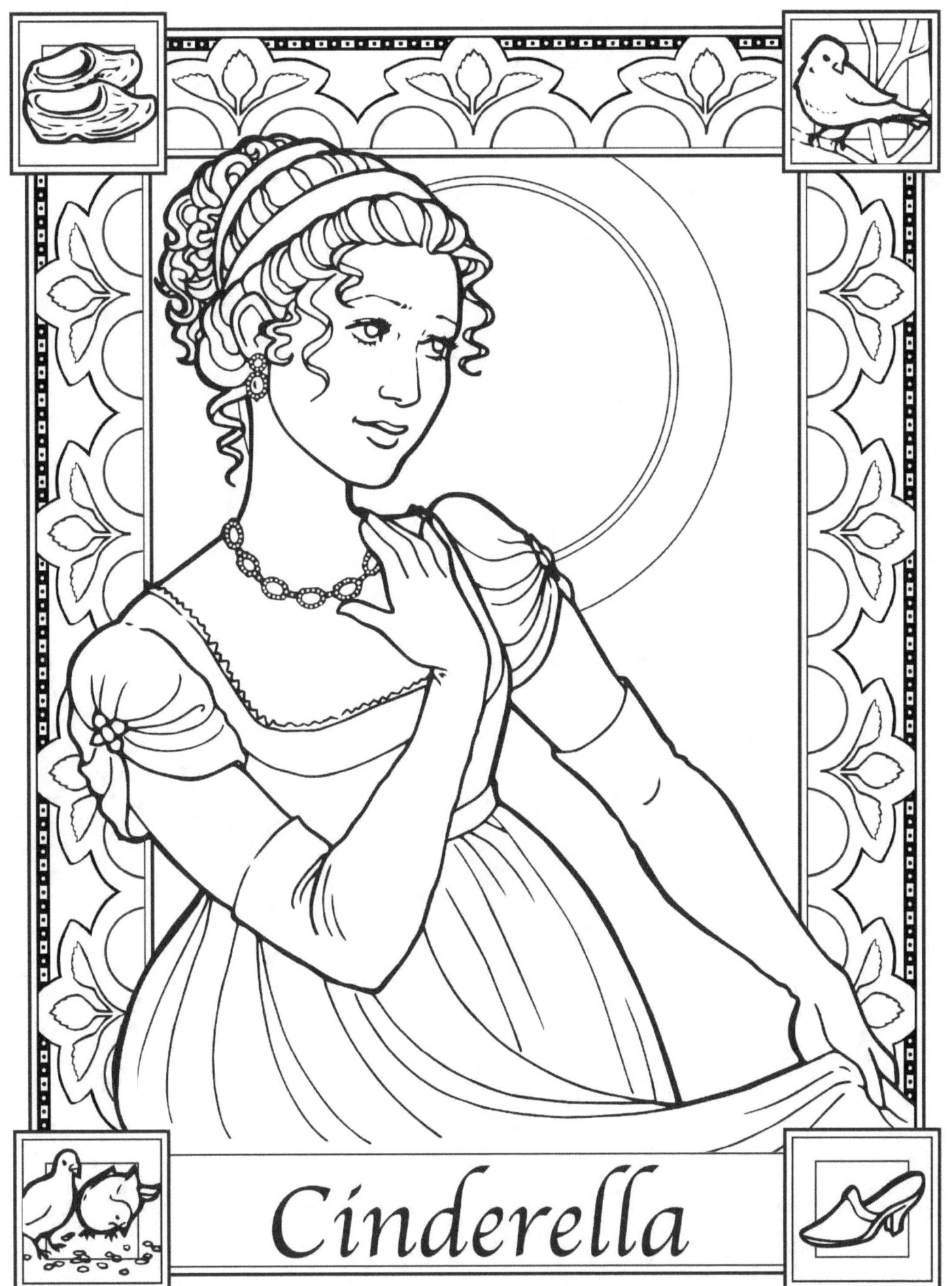

Cinderella

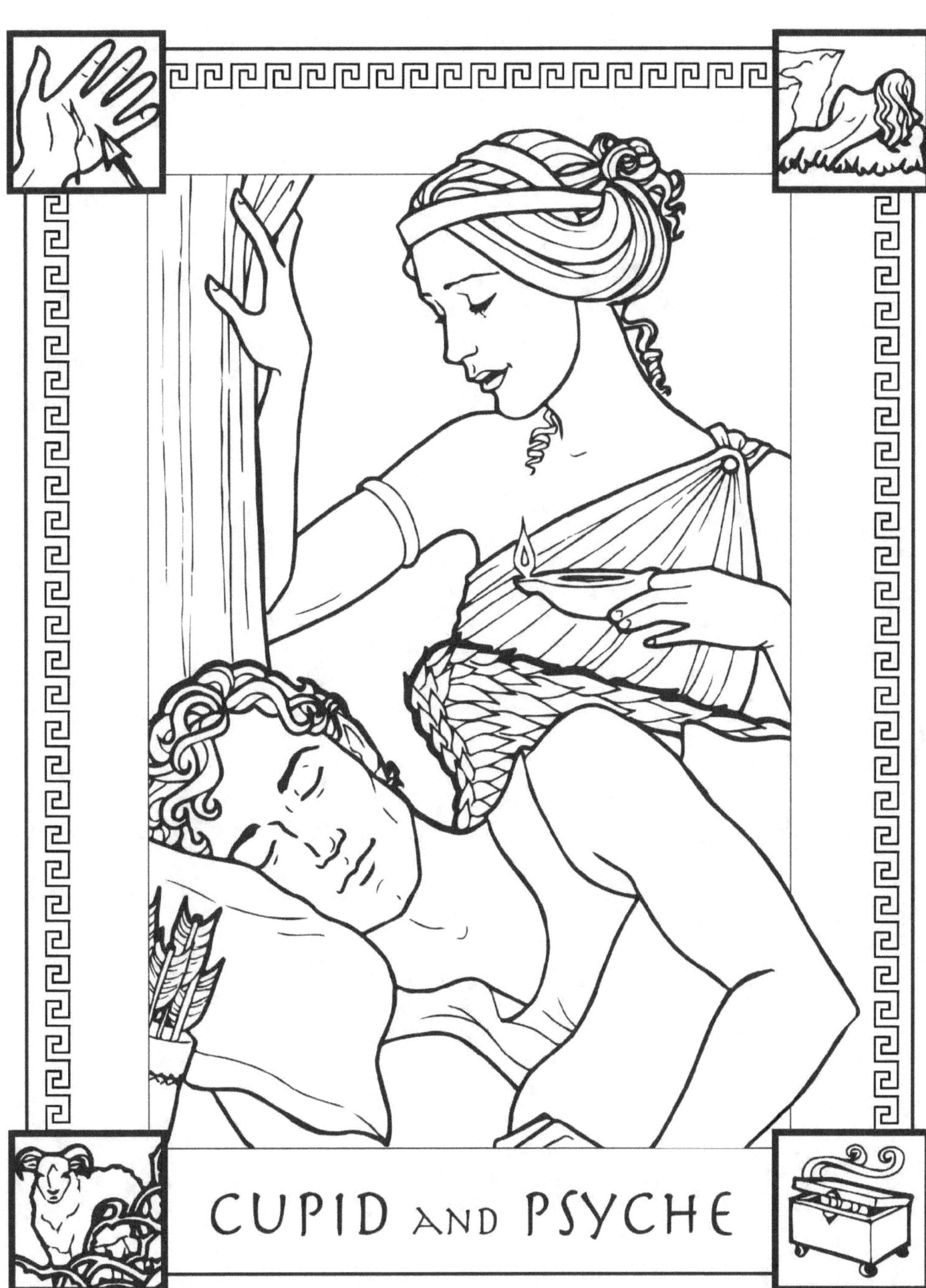

CUPID AND PSYCHE

Goldilocks

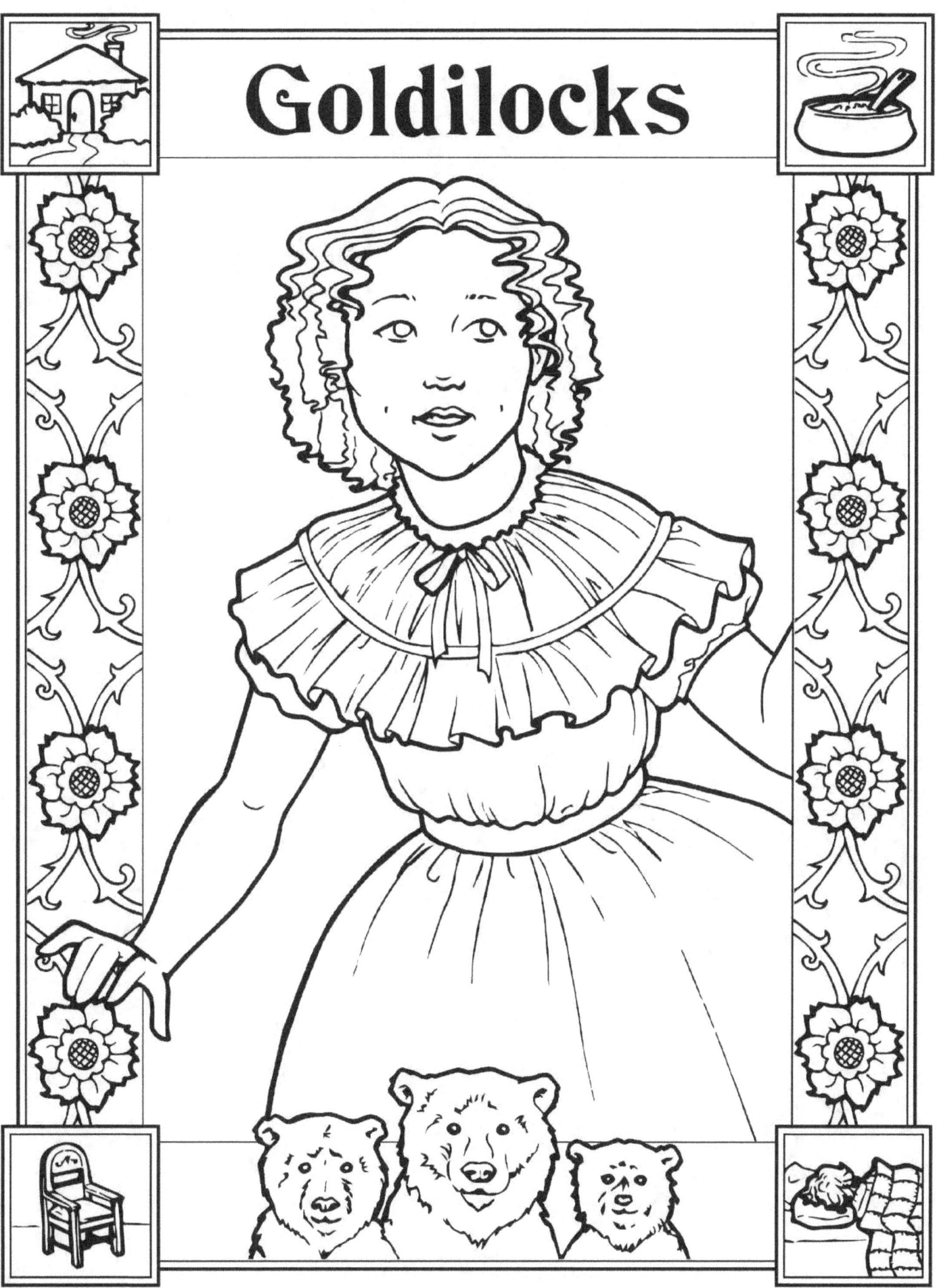

· Guinevere ·

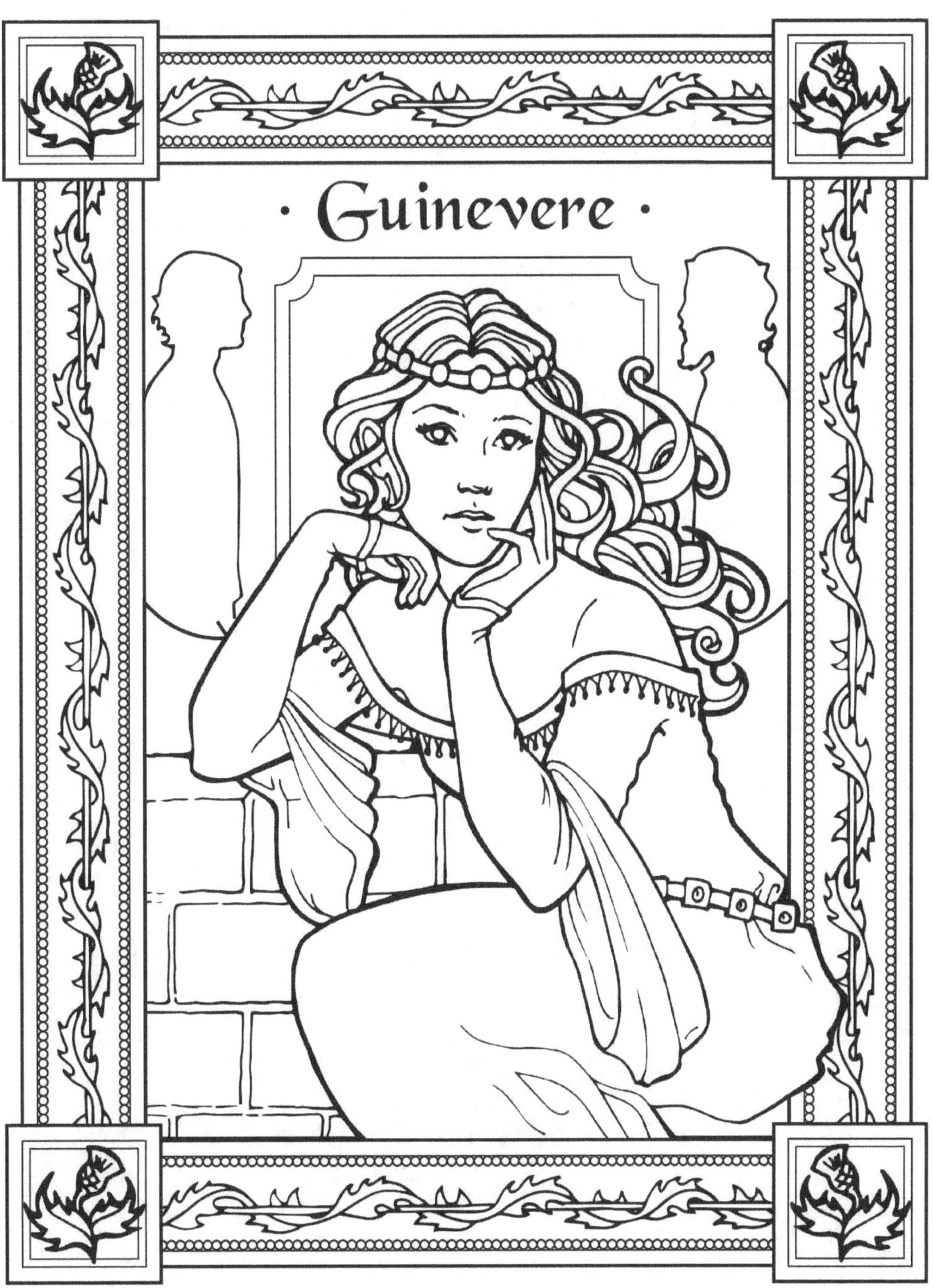

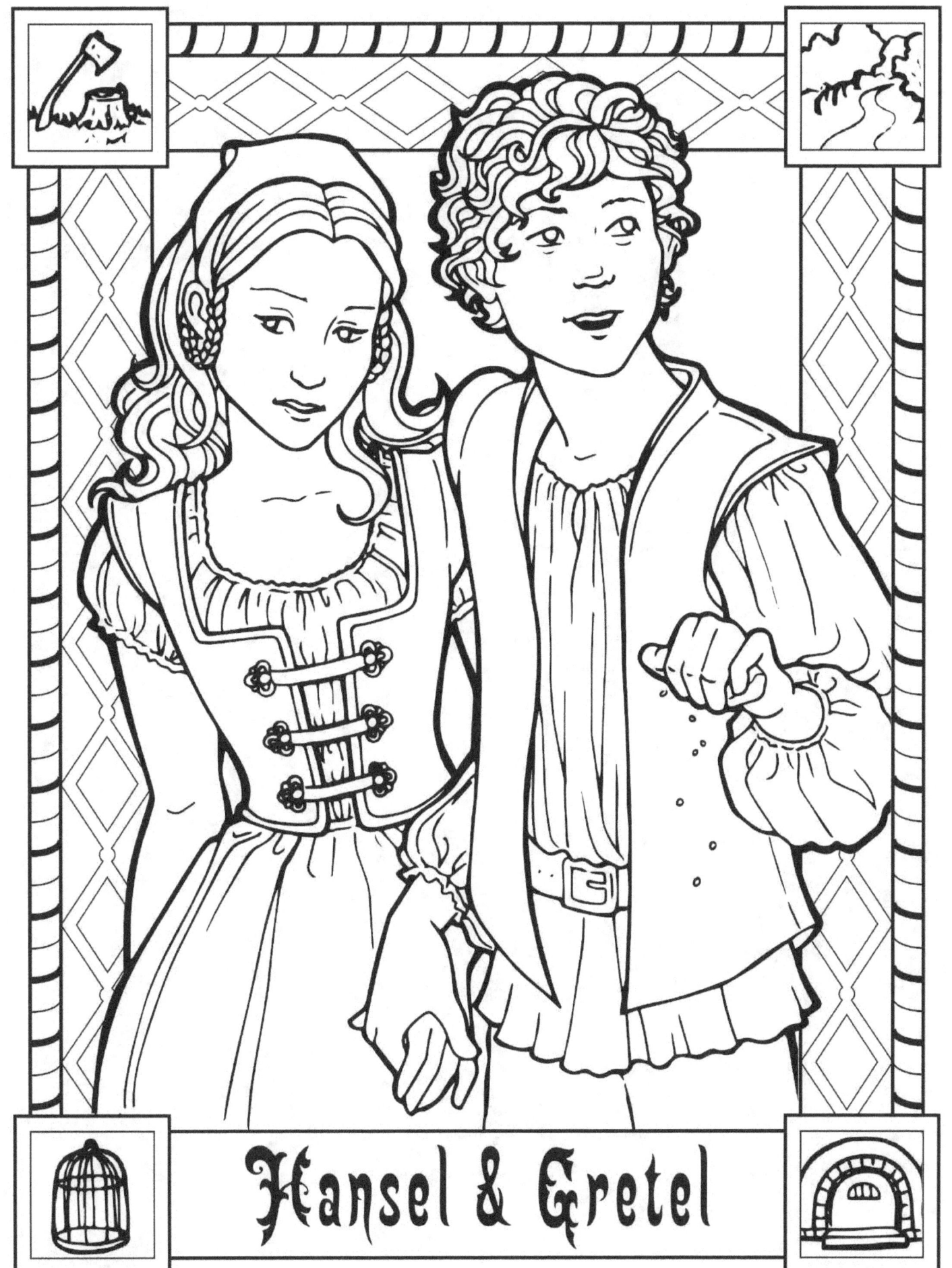

Hansel & Gretel

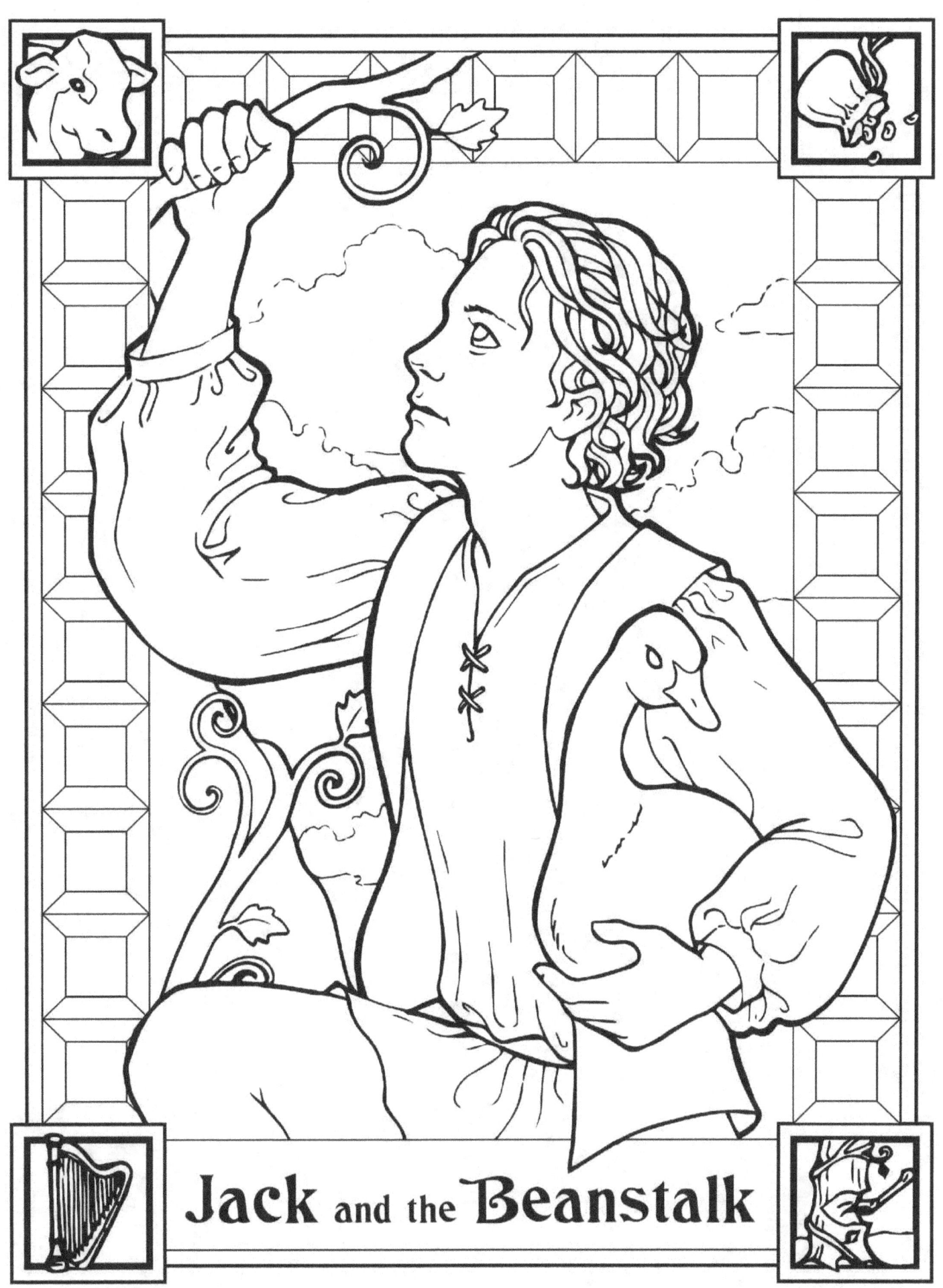

Jack and the Beanstalk

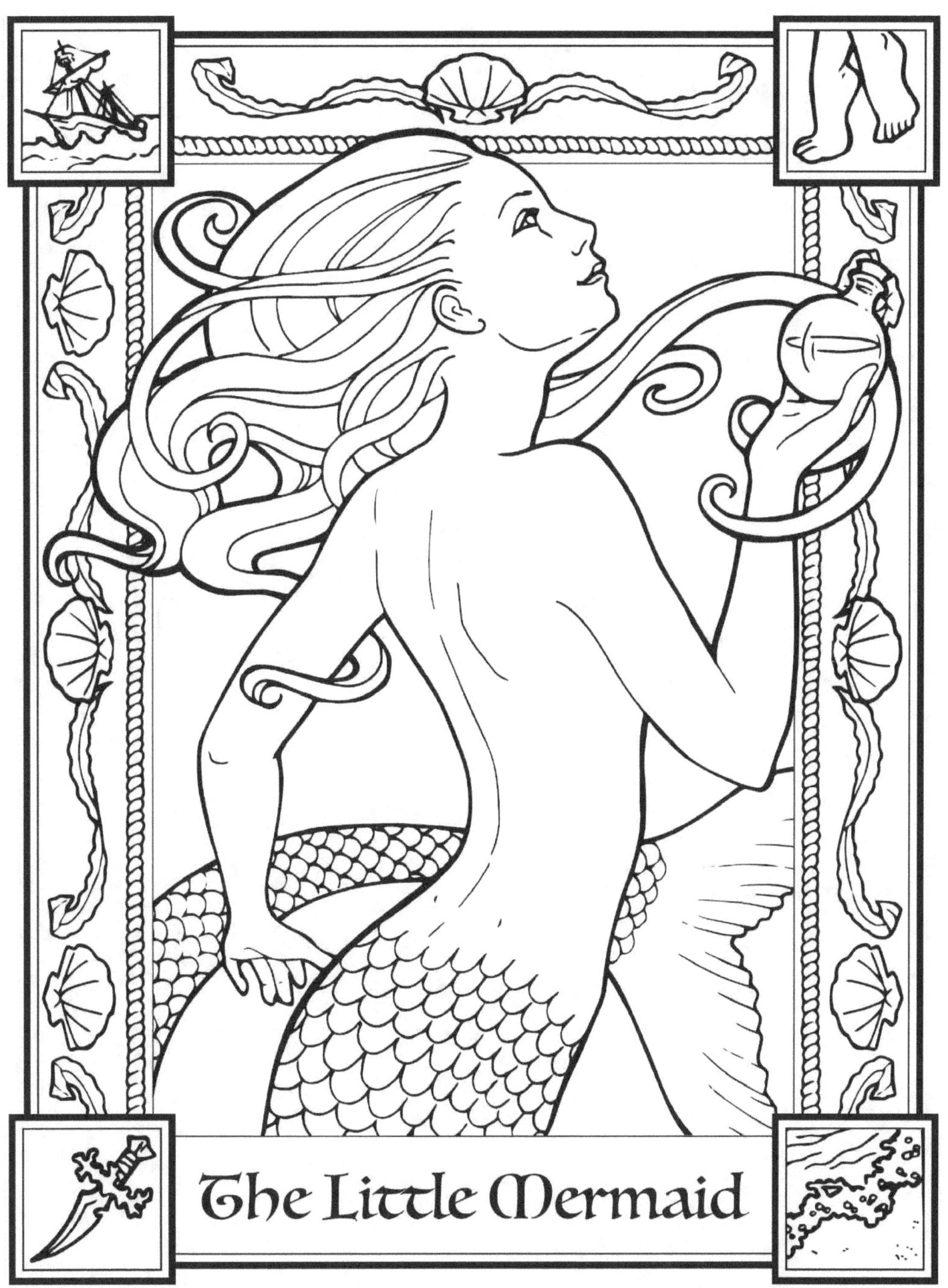

The Little Mermaid

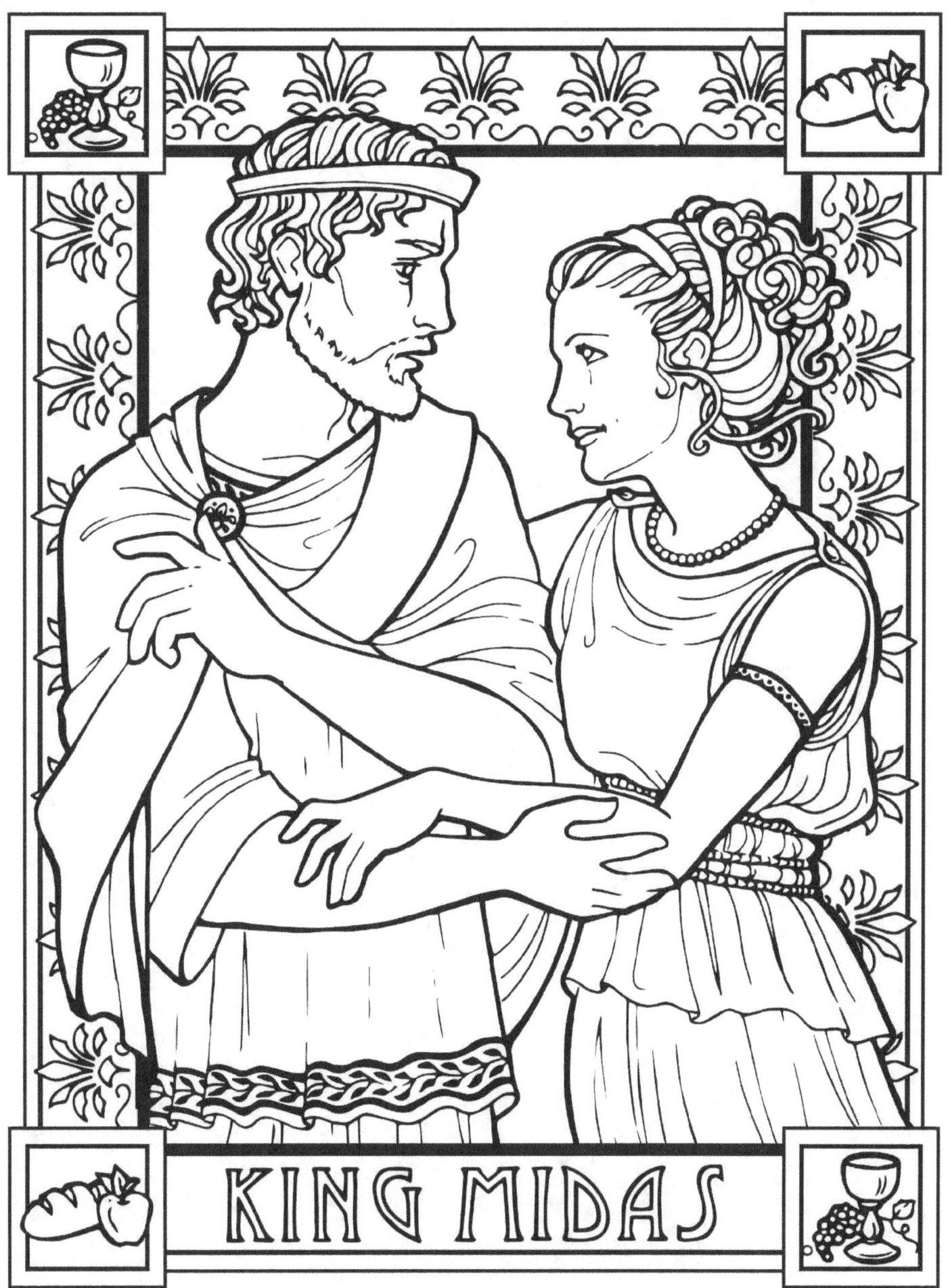

KING MIDAS

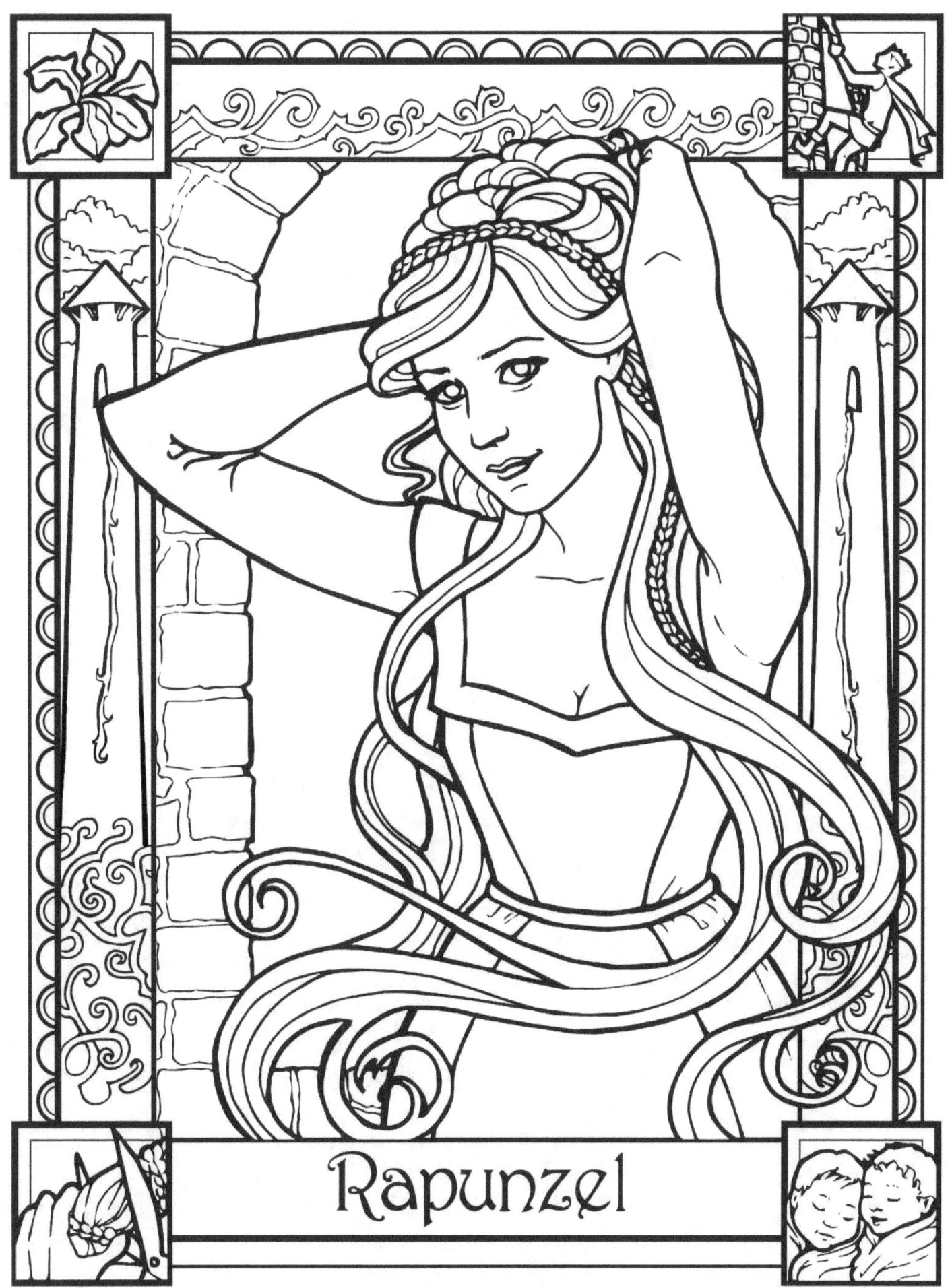

Rapunzel

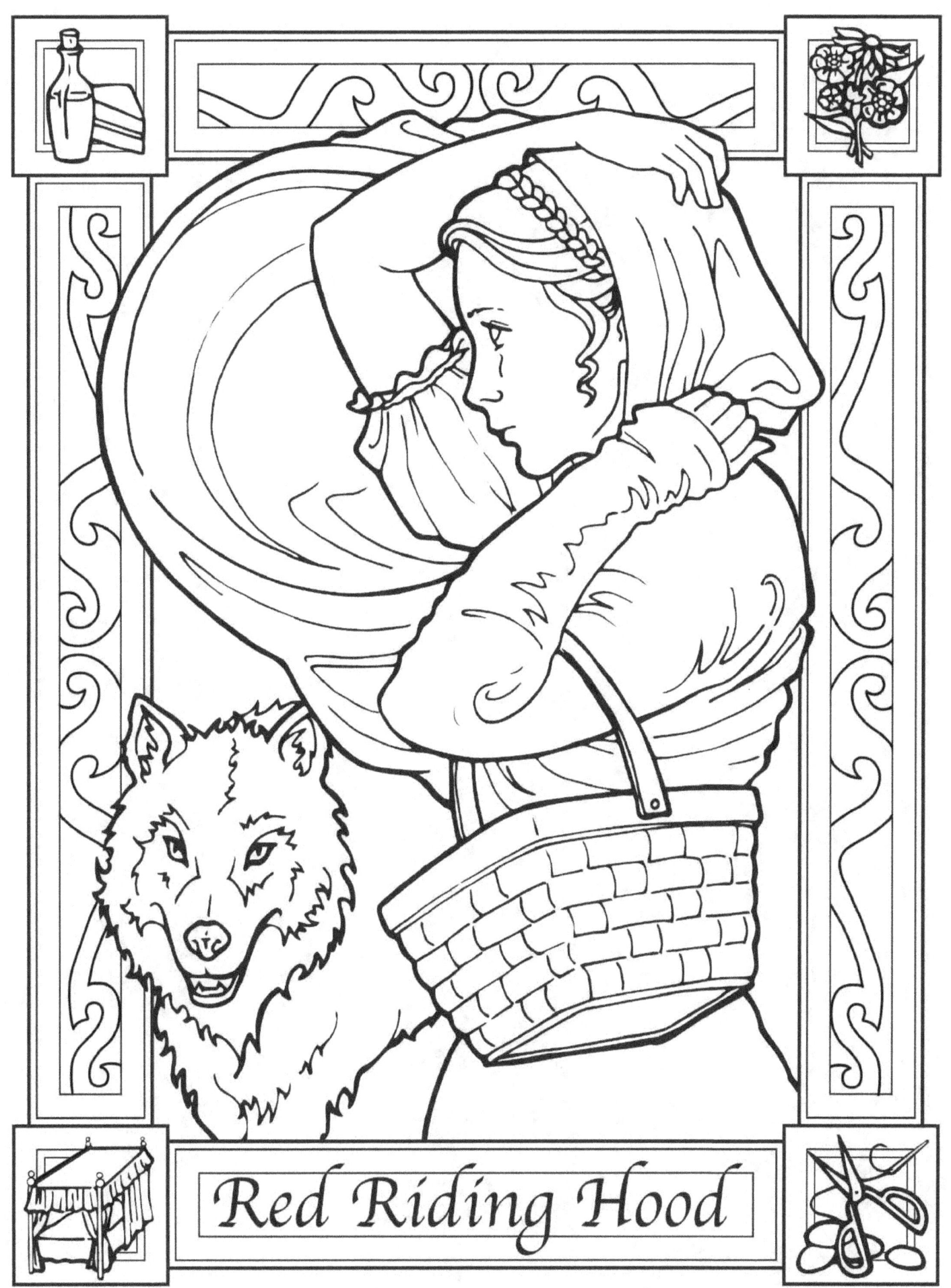

Red Riding Hood

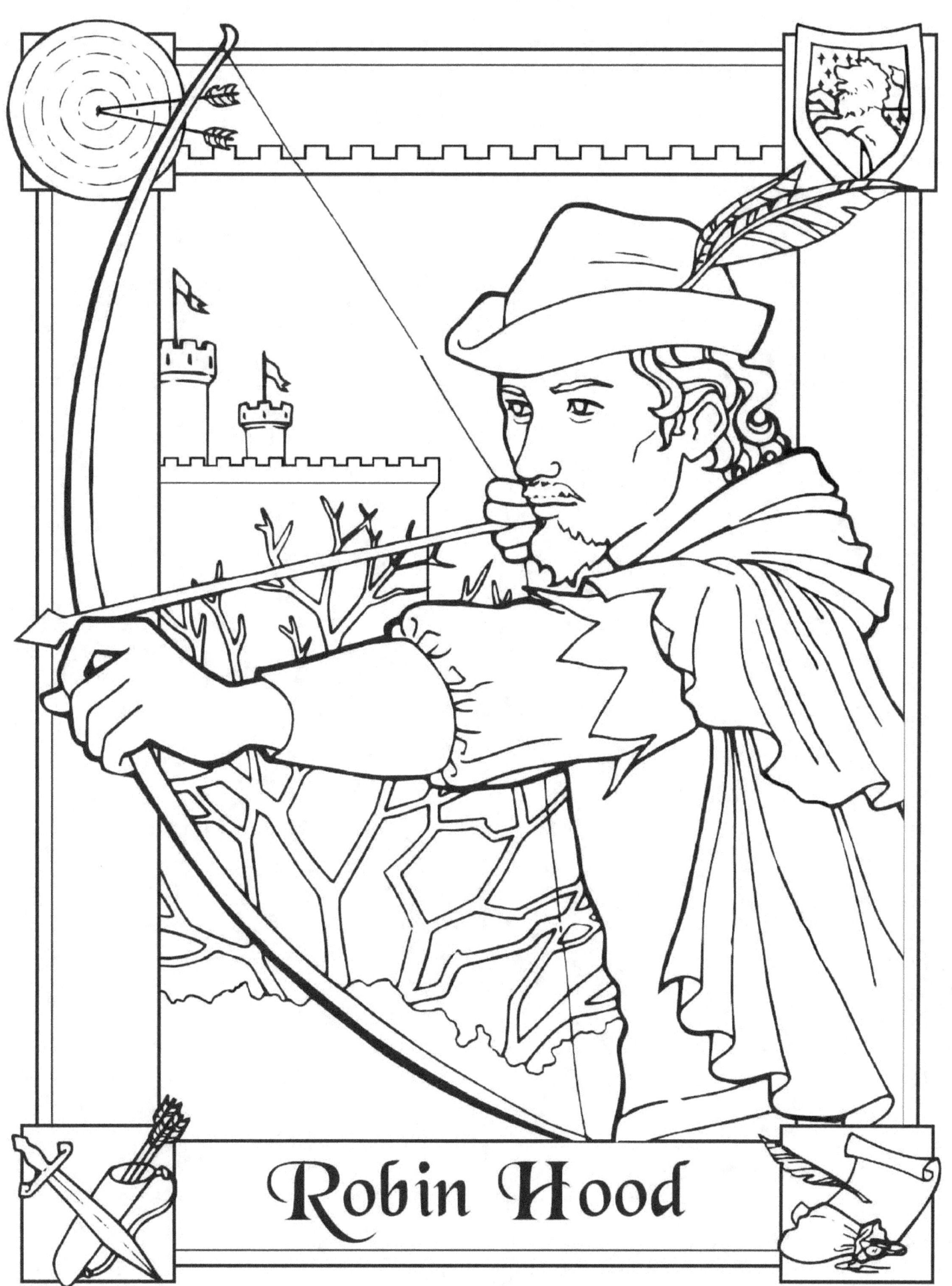

Robin Hood

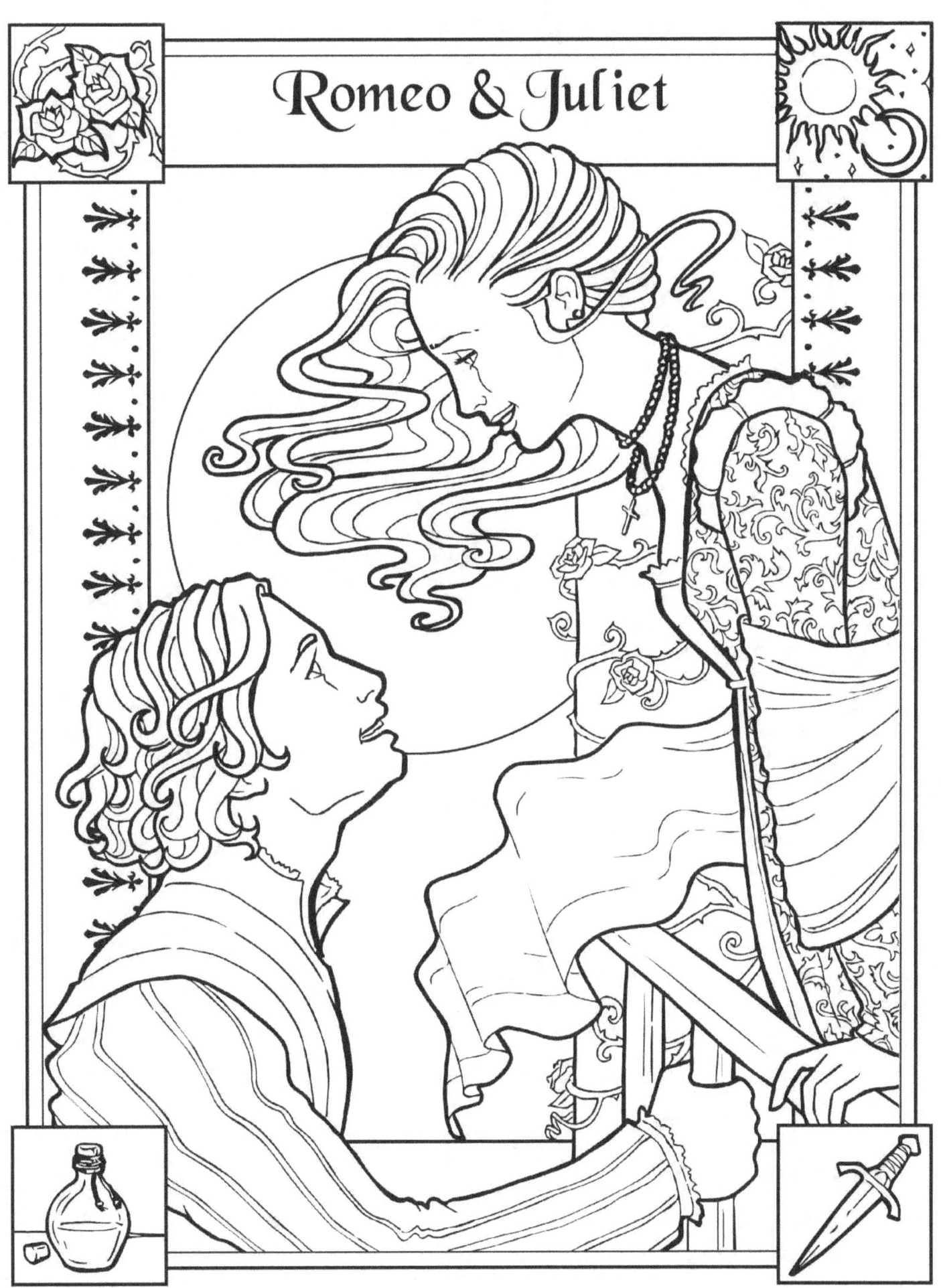

Romeo & Juliet

Rumplestiltskin

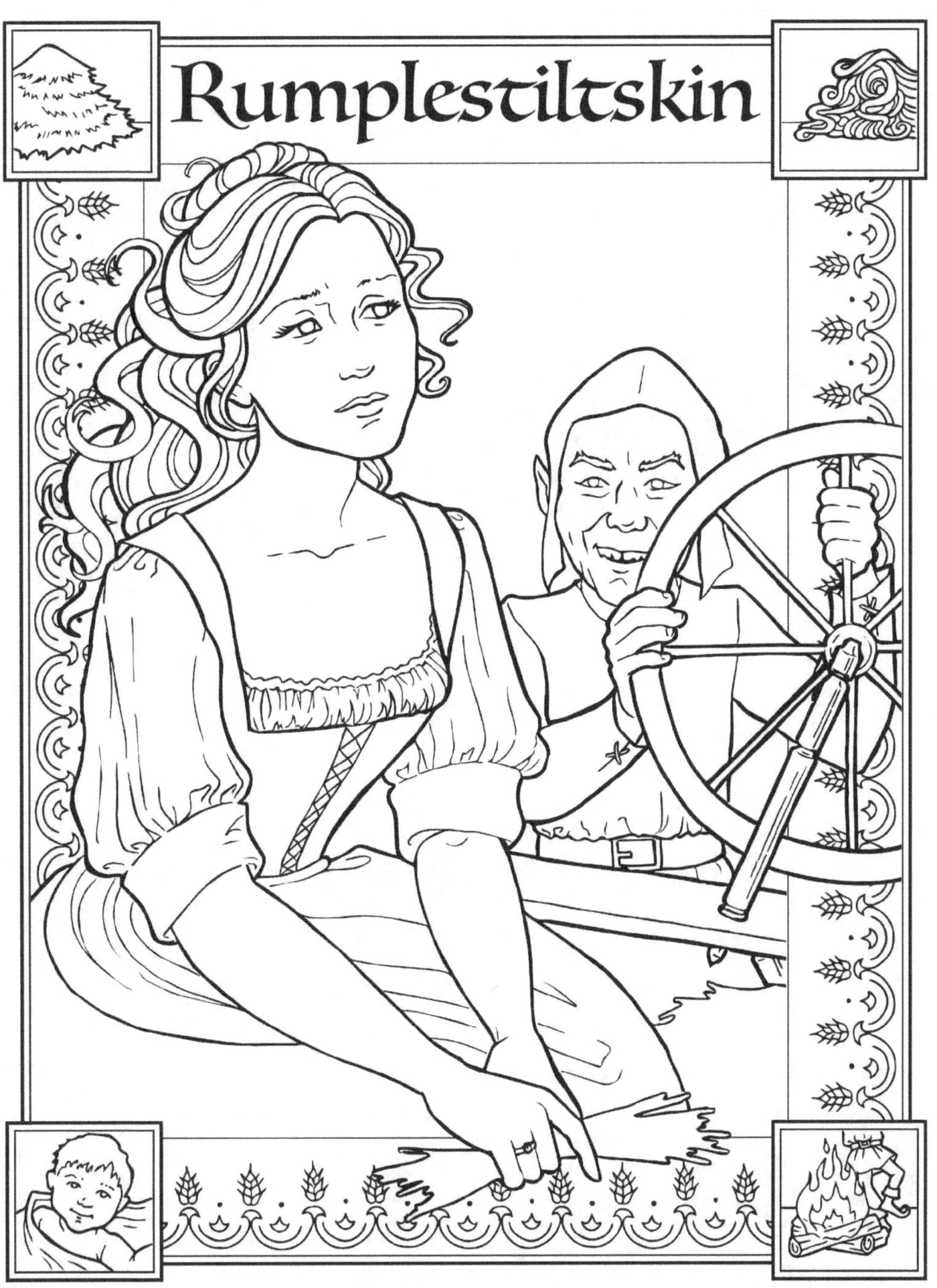

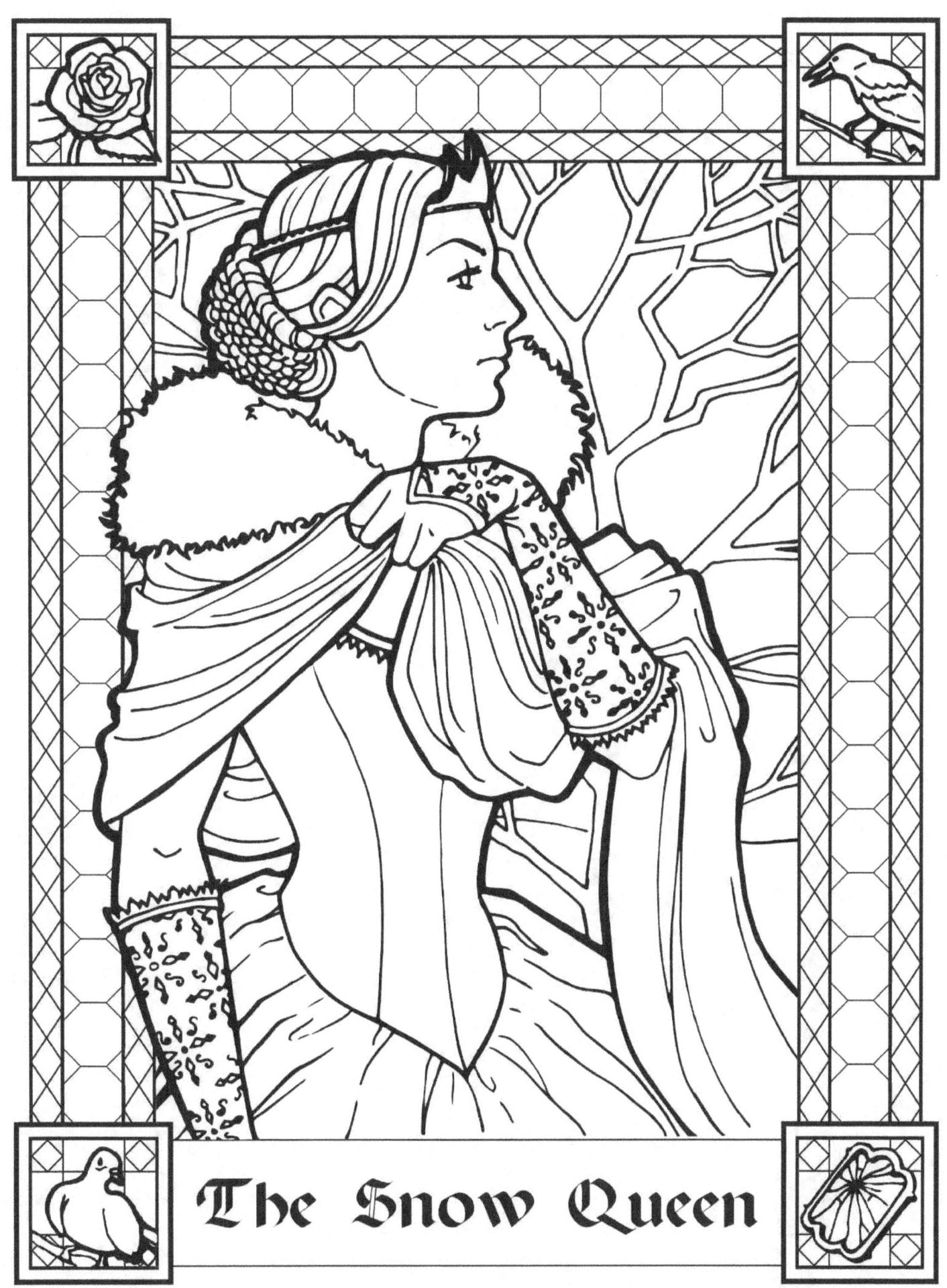

The Snow Queen

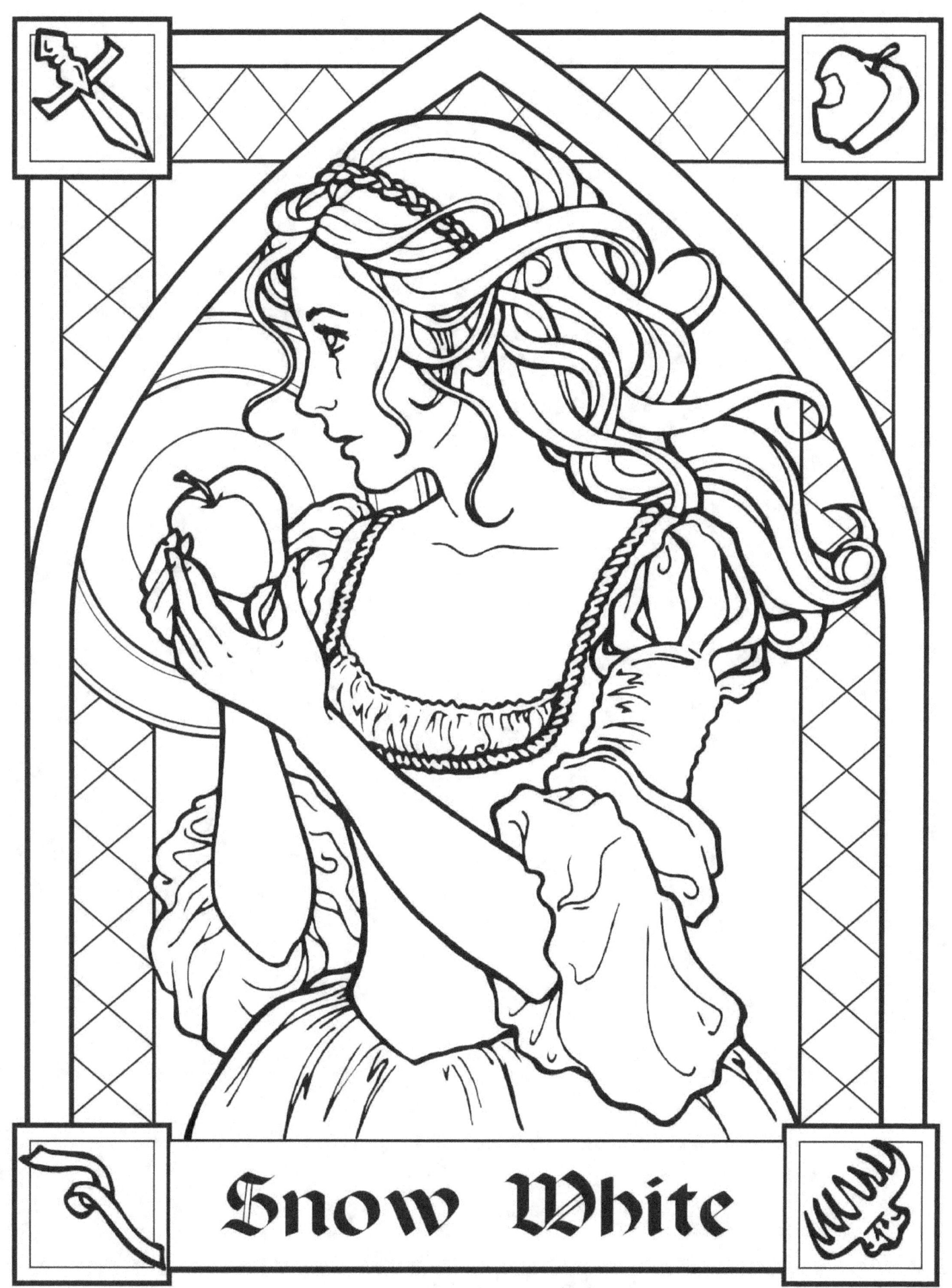

Snow White

Snow White

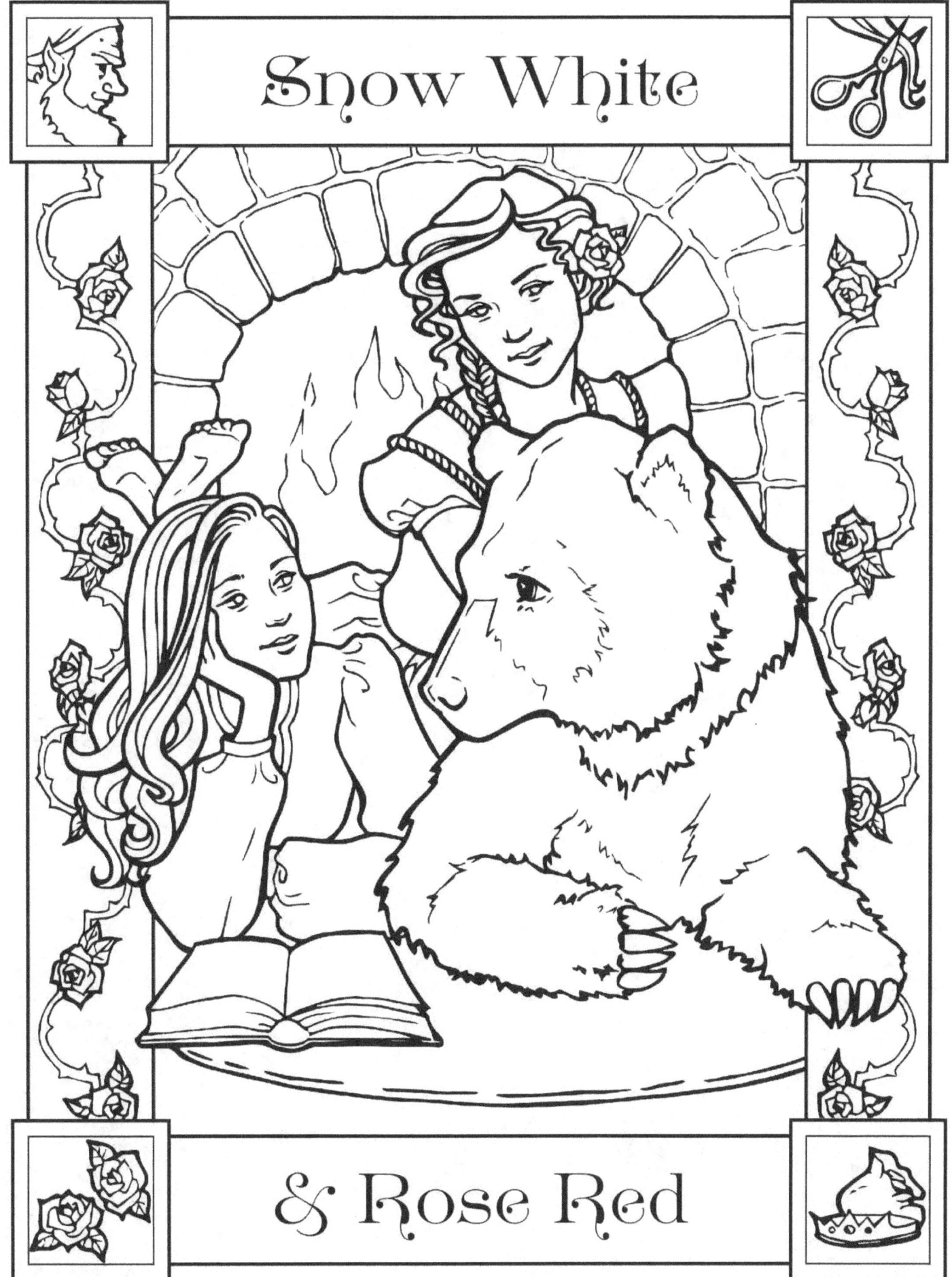

& Rose Red

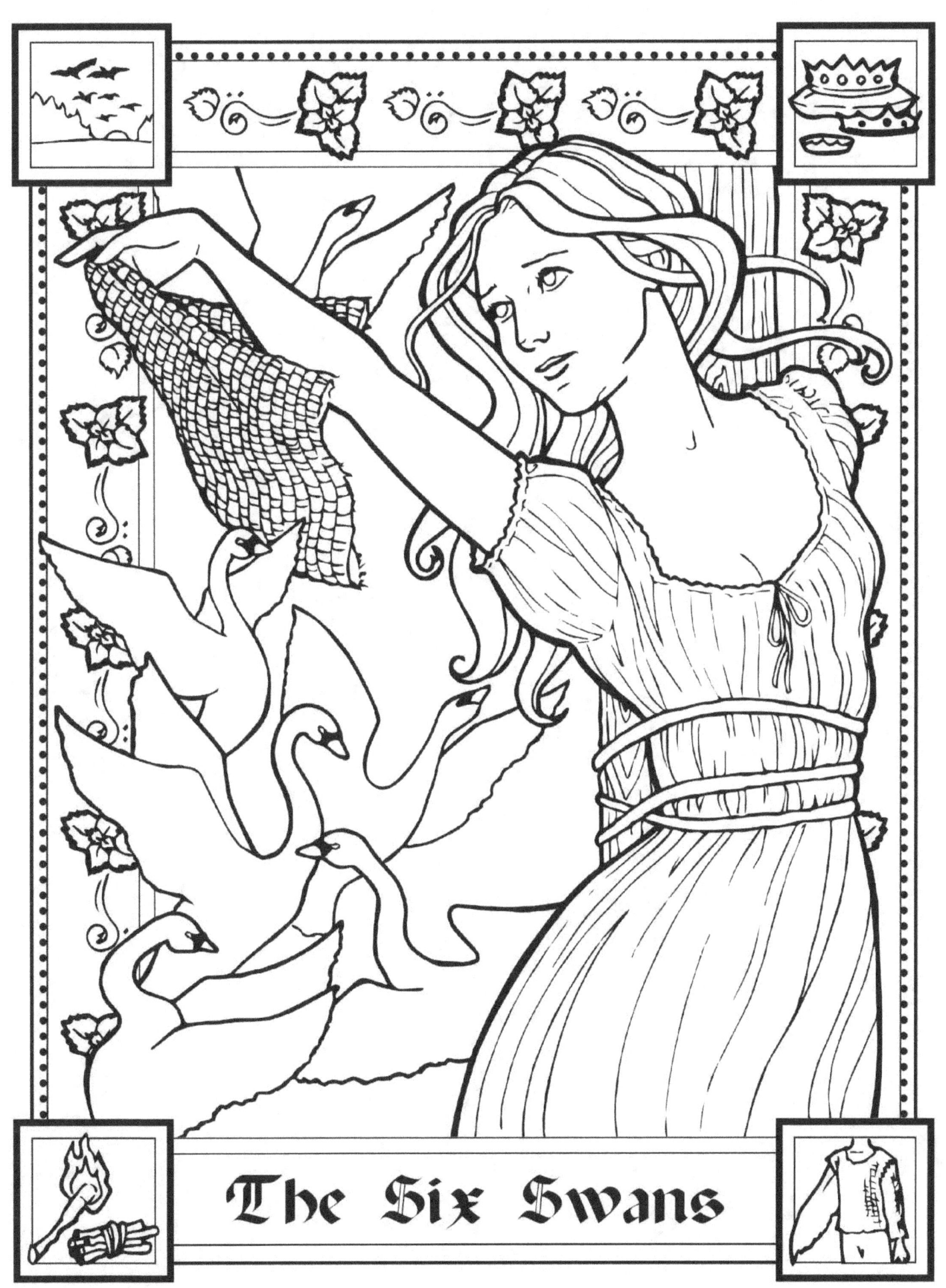

The Six Swans